KS3 ENGLISH IS EASY

(WRITING – THE BASICS)

THE
REVISION
SERIES

www.How2Become.com

As part of this product you have also received FREE access to online tests that will help you to pass Key Stage 3 ENGLISH *(Writing – The Basics)*.

To gain access, simply go to:

www.PsychometricTestsOnline.co.uk

Get more products
for passing any test at:

www.How2Become.com

Orders: Please contact How2Become Ltd, Suite 14, 50 Churchill Square Business Centre, Kings Hill, Kent ME19 4YU.

You can order through Amazon.co.uk under ISBN 9781911259022, via the website www.How2Become.com or through Gardners.com.

ISBN: 9781911259022

First published in 2016 by How2Become Ltd.

Copyright © 2016 How2Become.

Typeset for How2Become Ltd by Anton Pshinka.

Disclaimer

Every effort has been made to ensure that the information contained within this guide is accurate at the time of publication. How2Become Ltd is not responsible for anyone failing any part of any selection process as a result of the information contained within this guide. How2Become Ltd and their authors cannot accept any responsibility for any errors or omissions within this guide, however caused. No responsibility for loss or damage occasioned by any person acting, or refraining from action, as a result of the material in this publication can be accepted by How2Become Ltd.

The information within this guide does not represent the views of any third party service or organisation.

CONTENTS

**THE
REVISION
SERIES**

UNDERSTANDING THE CURRICULUM

THE NATIONAL CURRICULUM

State-funded schools use a curriculum of 'core' subjects, to form their students' timetables. These core subjects are essential for providing key knowledge and skills; which in turn will help us to produce well-rounded and educated citizens.

In Key Stage 3 (ages 11-14), the core subjects that must be taught in schools include the following:

- **English**
- **Maths**
- **Science**
- **Art and Design**
- **Citizenship**
- **Computing**
- **Design and Technology**
- **Languages**
- **Geography**
- **History**
- **Music**
- **Physical Education**

From Key Stage 1 to Key Stage 4, all schools must also teach Religious Studies to their students; and from the age of 11, children will also be taught Sex Education. However, parents are given the option of pulling their children out from Religious Studies and Sex Education.

THE IMPORTANCE OF ENGLISH

Students are taught the importance of English via spoken language, reading, writing and vocabulary. Not only is this a core subject which all students are required to undertake, but this subject is an integral part of other school subjects. Children will need to have a strong grasp of the English Language, and this will prove vital if they are to be successful across their school subjects.

<u>The fundamental aims of the English subject include:</u>

- Helping students to read with fluency and ease;
- Demonstrating a good understanding of the English Language;
- Highlighting the importance of reading, and allowing students to read for both pleasure and academia;
- Learning how to appreciate the English Language and its heritage;
- Acquiring a strong English vocabulary, to improve students' reading, writing and listening skills;
- Teaching students how to adapt their writing and language, in order to meet a specific purpose, context and audience;
- Improving children's confidence in their English abilities, allowing them to become competent in the English Language via verbal and written communication.

At Key Stage 3, the English subject focuses on four main 'disciplines':

- **Reading**
- **Writing**
- **Grammar and Vocabulary**
- **Spoken English**

The aforementioned disciplines are all used to teach students vital skills for both academia and the outside world.

READING AND WRITING

Reading and writing form the very basic skills that every person should obtain from an early age.

Reading is great for students, since it allows them to read for pleasure as well as for information. The ability to read is also necessary across other school subjects, and therefore it is important that students are able to read fluently and effectively.

Writing is a great skill which can be altered to reflect different contexts, purposes and audiences. In Key Stage 3, students are required to write different literary texts, for different purposes. Thus, strong knowledge of vocabulary and grammar is needed.

GRAMMAR AND VOCABULARY

Students in Key Stage 3 will need to extend knowledge which was obtained in Key Stage 2.

Teachers will need to enhance students' proficiency by teaching them the importance of grammar, punctuation and spelling. These key areas allow students to not only analyse literary texts, but to also improve their own writing style.

Linguistically, students will need to develop a strong understanding of English terminology, and learn how this can be applied to literary texts. This includes learning the ability to use appropriate vocabulary, understanding the meaning of words and phrases, and learning how to analyse, practice and apply literary techniques in their own work.

SPOKEN ENGLISH

Not only is written communication an important aspect of the English Language, but the ability to speak fluent English is just as vital.

Spoken English is used every day, in a range of different contexts. Developing a person's speaking skills will allow for well-rounded citizens, who have the ability to communicate effectively.

Speaking skills allow students to become more confident at speaking out loud, and to engage with the English Language competently.

Having a strong understanding of the English Language will allow students to become fluent in written and spoken English. This will allow them to communicate effectively with the world around them, thus allowing children to become engaged in cultural, social and economic issues, as well as intellectual debates.

ENGLISH SUBJECT CONTENT

Below we have broken down the aims and objectives of each 'discipline' for the subject. This will hopefully give you some idea of what will be assessed, and how you can improve different areas in your reading, writing and speaking abilities.

READING

Pupils will be taught how to:

- Develop an appreciation of the English language.
- Engage with a variety of literary texts including:
    - *Non-fiction, fiction, plays and poetry. Texts that cover a wide range of genres, eras, authors, styles and narratives.*
    - *Reading books for pleasure and academia.*
    - *Understanding the importance of Shakespeare's works.*
- Engage with challenging texts by:
    - *Learning new vocabulary, grammar and literary techniques.*
    - *Analysing key words and phrases.*
    - *Making inferences and assumptions based on the information provided.*
    - *Knowing the meaning behind the text, including the purpose, audience and context.*
- Read critically:
    - *Recognising different literary techniques.*
    - *Analysing narration, characterisation, style, themes and genre.*
    - *Comparing two or more texts (cross-examination).*
    - *Understanding meaning through figurative language, word choices, structure and conventions.*

WRITING

<u>Pupils will be taught how to:</u>

❑ Write with fluency, ease and control.
❑ Write a range of different literary texts including:
- *Strong, persuasive, narrative essays.*
- *Short stories, plays and poetry.*
- *Imaginative writing.*
- *Formal letters.*
- *Scripts and presentations.*

❑ Plan, draft and proofread writing:
- *Plan and draft your ideas. Think about:*
  - *Characters, narrative, themes, motives, style, context, audience and purpose.*
- *Carefully choosing grammar and understanding the importance of vocabulary.*
- *Structuring your writing format in a clear and concise manner.*
- *Understanding the importance of audience, and how your writing can be influential.*

❑ Be original and creative.
❑ Use the English language in a way that is expressive, creative, informative, imaginative or personal.

SPOKEN ENGLISH

<u>Pupils will be taught how to:</u>

❑ Verbally communicate to a high standard by:
- *Speaking confidently, persuasively and effectively.*

❑ Improve their speaking skills by engaging with particular grammar and vocabulary:
- *Understanding what type of spoken English they should use and in what context.*
- *Understanding how to get their point across in the best possible way.*

❑ Participate in verbal debates, discussions and presentations.
❑ Improve on speaking skills such as volume, tone, enthusiasm and interaction.

GRAMMAR AND VOCABULARY

Pupils will be taught how to:

❑ Improve on pre-existing grammar and vocabulary skills taught in Key Stage 2.
❑ Understand the importance of grammar:
  - *How this creates meaning.*
  - *The impact this has on the audience.*
❑ Analyse key words and phrases:
  - *Why they are used.*
  - *The meaning behind them.*
  - *What is the author implying/inferring?*
❑ Understand what grammar and vocabulary to use. Think about:
  - *What kind of literary text they are writing/reading.*
  - *What do words mean and how can they be interpreted?*
  - *Is it a formal or informal piece of literary text?*

English is not only a core subject, but a topic that impacts upon every aspect of our daily lives. As you can see, it is imperative that students are able to engage with the English Language, in order to improve on vital skills and knowledge.

USING THIS GUIDE

This guide focuses specifically on Key Stage 3 English Writing (The Basics). It will cover all of the basics, that every child will need to know, to ensure top marks across the English subject.

REMEMBER – It's really important that you have a good writing ability, as this will help across all school subjects.

HOW WILL I BE ASSESSED?

In Years 7, 8 and 9, children will be assessed based on Levels. These 3 years do not count towards any official grade, and are simply a reflection of progression and development. The first years of secondary school determine whether or not pupils are meeting the minimum requirements. These 3 years are integral for preparing pupils for their GCSEs.

Although these years do not count towards any final results, they do go a long way to deciphering which GCSEs you will pick up. For example, if you were excelling in Art and Design in KS3, you could consider taking this subject at GCSE.

The subjects that you choose at GCSE will impact upon your future aspirations, including further education and career opportunities.

You will be monitored and assessed throughout these schooling years, via the following:

- Ongoing teacher assessments;
- Term progress reports;
- Summative assessments at the end of each academic year.

By the end of Key Stage 3, pupils are expected to achieve Levels 5 or 6.

THE
REVISION
SERIES

INCREASE YOUR CHANCES

Below is a list of GOLDEN NUGGETS that will help YOU and your CHILD to prepare for the Key Stage 3 English exam.

Golden Nugget 1 – Revision timetables

When it comes to revising, preparation is key. That is why you need to sit down with your child and come up with an efficient and well-structured revision timetable.

It is important that you work with your child to assess their academic strengths and weaknesses, in order to carry out these revision sessions successfully.

> *TIP* – *Focus on their weaker areas first!*
>
> *TIP* – *Create a weekly revision timetable to work through different subject areas.*
>
> *TIP* – *Spend time revising with your child. Your child will benefit from your help and this is a great way for you to monitor their progress.*

Golden Nugget 2 – Understanding the best way your child learns

There are many different ways to revise when it comes to exams, and it all comes down to picking a way that your child will find most useful.

Below is a list of the common learning styles that you may want to try with your child:

- **Visual** – the use of pictures and images to remember information.

- **Aural** – the use of sound and music to remember information.

- **Verbal** – the use of words, in both speech and writing, to understand information.

- **Social** – working together in groups.

- **Solitary** – working and studying alone.

Popular revision techniques include: *mind mapping, flash cards, making notes, drawing flow charts,* and *diagrams*. You could instruct your child on how to turn diagrams and pictures into words, and words into diagrams. Try as many different methods as possible, to see which style your child learns from the most.

> ***TIP*** *– Work out what kind of learner your child is. What method will they benefit from the most?*
>
> ***TIP*** *– Try a couple of different learning aids and see if you notice a change in your child's ability to understand what is being taught.*

Golden Nugget 3 – Break times

Allow your child plenty of breaks when revising.

It's really important not to overwork your child.

> ***TIP*** *– Practising for 10 to 15 minutes per day will improve your child's writing ability.*
>
> ***TIP*** *– Keep in mind that a child's retention rate is usually between 30 to 50 minutes. Any longer than this, and your child will start to lose interest.*

Golden Nugget 4 – Practice, practice and more practice!

Purchase past practice papers. Although the curriculum will have changed for 2016, practice papers are still a fantastic way for you to gain an idea of how your child is likely to be tested.

Golden Nugget 5 – Variety is key!

Make sure that your child practices writing a VARIETY of different literary texts. Broadening their understanding of different genres, styles and formats will help them to prepare effectively for writing different literature.

> *TIP – Make sure you practice different writing skills. Practice writing different literary styles including fiction, non-fiction, plays and poetry.*

Golden Nugget 6 – Improve their confidence

Encourage your child to communicate verbally, as well as in their writing. This will allow them to improve their confidence and their English ability.

> *TIP – Have discussions and debates in order to encourage your child to open up and discuss their work.*
>
> *TIP – Try and get your child to deliver presentations to family members and friends. This will really help to improve their confidence.*

Golden Nugget 7 – Stay positive!

The most important piece of preparation advice we can give you, is to make sure that your child is positive and relaxed about these tests.

Don't let assessments worry you, and certainly don't let them worry your child.

> *TIP – Make sure the home environment is as comfortable and relaxed as possible for your child.*

Golden Nugget 8 – Answer the easier questions first

A good tip to teach your child is to answer all the questions they find easiest first. That way, they can swiftly work through the paper, before attempting the questions they struggle with.

TIP – Get your child to undergo a practice paper. Tell them to fill in the answers that they find the easiest first. That way, you can spend time helping your child with the questions they find more difficult.

Spend some time working through the questions they find difficult and make sure that they know how to work out the answer.

Golden Nugget 9 – Make sure they use the P.E.E. technique

The biggest advice we can give to you and your child is to make sure the P.E.E. technique is used when writing. When writing, always try to write by making a point, providing examples/evidence, and then explaining your answer in more detail. This will help to strengthen the overall responses to the questions being asked.

Golden Nugget 10 – Understanding key terms

The next section is a glossary containing all the KEY TERMS that your child should familiarise themselves with.

Sit down with your child and learn as many of these KEY TERMS as you can.

TIP – Why not make your child's learning fun? Write down all of the key terms and cut them out individually. Do the same for the definitions.

Get your child to try and match the KEY TERM with its definition. Keep playing this game until they get them all right!

Golden Nugget 11 – Check out our other revision resources

We have a range of other English resources to help you prepare for EVERY element of KS3 English.

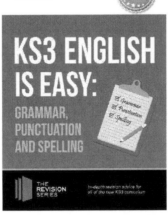

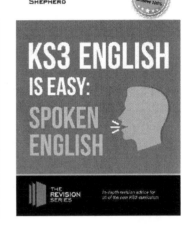

ACTIVE	A sentence in which the subject acts.
ALLITERATION	The repetition of the same sound or letter, used at the beginning of adjacent or closely connected words.
AMBIGUOUS	Having more than one possible interpretation.
AUDIENCE	The people who view the text.
AUTHOR	The writer or creator of that particular literary text.
CHARACTERISATION	The way in which an actor (in a play) acts out their role. Bringing a character to life.
CLIMAX	The moment the text reaches its greatest danger or suspense. Often the main crisis.
COLLOQUIAL	Popular informal writing (colloquialism).
COMPARISON	Similarities and differences between different texts.
CONTEXT	Historical or cultural context. Understanding the context behind the written text.
DERIVATION	Where something (a word) comes from.
DIALOGUE	Spoken speech (a conversation) between two or more people.
DRAFTING	Preparing a first (preliminary) version of a document. This may require proofreading and editing (see definitions).
EDITING	Modifying literary work in order to make it read more effectively.
EVIDENCE	A way of supporting your answers by using ACTUAL proof from the passage.
FACT	True pieces of information.
FICTION	A literary style in the form of prose (novels). These events and people are imaginary – it is invented / not from real life.

FIGURATIVE LANGUAGE	A figure of speech that goes beyond the literal meaning. *For example, metaphors, similes, hyperbole, personification etc.*
FORMAL WRITING	Formal writing is a style of complex, longer sentences which are used in more professional writing.
IMAGERY	Visually descriptive or figurative language.
IMAGINATIVE WRITING	Imaginative writing is creative writing. This is quite often shown in fiction texts (where authors make up their own story).
INFORMAL WRITING	Informal writing is simple and often uses colloquial language – as if you were talking to friends and family.
IRONY	Suggesting a meaning by saying the opposite of what is actually meant.
LANGUAGE	The words and vocabulary used in a literary text.
NARRATIVE	The storyline and/or meaning of a text.
NON-FICTION	Writing that is based on true / real-life events or facts. It provides the reader with real and factual information.
PARAGRAPHS	A way of breaking up text, in order for the passage to flow better. Each paragraph usually deals with a different theme or idea. Indicated by a new or indented line.
PASSIVE	A sentence in which the subject is acted on.
PATHOS	Emotional appeal.
P.E.E. TECHNIQUE	Point, Evidence, Explanation.
PLAYS	A type of literary style which involves dialogue between characters. Often intended for theatrical productions.

POETRY	A style of literary work which is based on feelings and ideas; using styles, rhythms, verses and composition.
PRESENTATION	The way something is portrayed to its readers / audience.
PROOFREADING	To read through literary work and correct any changes that need to be made.
PROSE	A natural flow of written or verbal speech.
PURPOSE	The reasons why a text was written. Is it to entertain, to inform, to instruct, to persuade?
RHYTHM	A strong pattern of a beat, which you can hear in words.
STANDARD ENGLISH	A form of English used widely and understood by most.
STRUCTURE	The way a literary text is laid out. The structure of a text will depend on what *type* of text it is (i.e. newspaper articles).
SYMBOLISM	The use of symbols to represent an idea or quality.
TENSE	When something was written. For example, is it written in the past, present or future tense?
THIRD PERSON	Style of narrative which is omniscient (e.g. he or she).
TONE	The mood created by particular language.
TRADITIONAL LITERATURE	The oldest type of literature. Stories passed down from generation to generation.
WRITING TO ADVISE	Offer suggestions and recommendations about something.
WRITING TO ARGUE	Offering alternative viewpoints about a topic. Influencing your reader to believe in what you are saying.

WRITING TO EXPLAIN	Show the meaning or account of something. Providing clarification.
WRITING TO INFORM	Telling readers something by providing information. Generally this doesn't offer opinions.
WRITING TO PERSUADE	Influencing your readers by persuading them to change their views, buy something, or consider something in a different perspective.

UNDERSTANDING THE QUESTION

(Drafting your Response)

UNDERSTANDING THE QUESTION

Before you begin writing, you need to make sure that you understand what the questions are asking you.

> It is common for people to just start writing, however this will do you no favours!

READ THE QUESTION CAREFULLY

Particularly for exams, people tend to rush through their answers, scared that they are going to run out of time. When they do this, they fail to read what is actually being asked of them.

<u>Consider the following before writing your response:</u>

- *What is the question asking you to do?*
- *Is the question asking more than one thing?*
- *How do you need to structure your response?*
- *What kind of style should your writing use?*
- *What kind of language should you use in your response?*

Reading the question carefully will ensure that you respond to what is being asked.

UNDERSTANDING THE QUESTION

LOOK AT WHAT IS BEING ASKED

More often than not, your writing will need to reflect the views of someone else.

For example, a question may ask you to imagine yourself as a businessman, or a teacher, or a character from a book. If that is the case, the language you would use would be very different to your own.

You may be asked to write something to someone. For example, you may be asked to write a letter to the council, or to a friend. The way you address a letter to the council would use very different language compared to a letter addressed to a friend.

TOP TIPS!

1. Spend some time reading the question.
2. Read the question 2 or 3 times to make sure you know what the question is *actually* asking.
3. Pick out KEY WORDS from the question.

WRITING AS A...	HOW TO STRUCTURE YOUR RESPONSE...
Teacher	Formal, professional language. Avoid colloquialism.
Children's author	Simple, easy-to-read language. Would not be as formal as an author of crime novels.
Journalist	Professional, intellectual language. Used to talk about a specific topic. Show strong knowledge.

WRITING TO A...	HOW TO STRUCTURE YOUR RESPONSE...
Businessman	Formal, professional language. Structured in a clear and precise manner.
Friend	Informal, colloquial language.
Parent	If the writing is coming from a child (to their parent), this could be informal. However, teachers addressing parents would use formal, professional language.

Question 1

You should scan over the question before you start writing...

a) Always

b) Sometimes

c) Never

Answer

Question 2

If you were writing a letter to your employer, what kind of language and format would you use?

_____

_____

_____

Question 3

Tick the appropriate boxes to show what kind of language you would use for a children's comic book.

FORMAL

TECHNICAL

INFORMAL

SIMPLE

DETAILED

Question 4

You have recently moved into a new house with your partner and a new-born baby. In the first couple of weeks, you have been left agitated by your neighbour's constant loud music, shouting outside, and rubbish left outside on the pavement.

Write the opening two paragraphs of a letter addressed to the council, explaining the disruptions and how you wish action to be taken.

Question 5

Some questions begin with a particular word, which tells you what it wants you to do. Match up the purpose of the question to the correct definition.

EXPLAIN	Carefully analyse the information provided.
ARGUE	Talk about a topic in detail.
EVALUATE	Offer alternative viewpoints about the same topic.
DISCUSS	Give a possibility/consideration about a topic.

ANSWERS TO UNDERSTANDING THE QUESTION

Question 1

C = Never

You should never scan over the question before writing. You need to read the question carefully – at least 2 or 3 times, in order to make sure you know what the question is asking you.

Question 2

If you were writing a letter to your employer, you would need to use professional, formal language. Proper sentence structure would be required in this letter. The letter would need to be laid out in a clear, easy-to-read, and professional manner.

Question 3

FORMAL	☐
TECHNICAL	☐
INFORMAL	✔
SIMPLE	✔
DETAILED	☐

Question 4

Your answer should be along the lines of the following:

I am writing this letter to discuss action to be taken against my neighbours. As a parent with a new-born baby, I am finding it extremely difficult to adjust to my neighbours' behaviour; including constant loud music, disruption and littering outside my house.

Would you be accepting of this type of behaviour if it was your next door neighbour? I bought this house with the intention to start afresh with my family. However, now I am starting to question whether or not I have made a terrible mistake.

Question 5

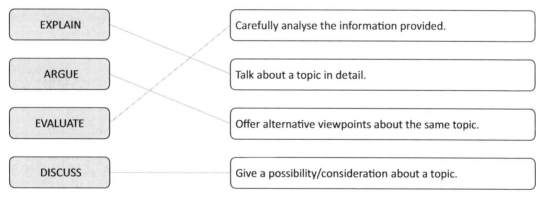

EXPLAIN	Carefully analyse the information provided.
ARGUE	Talk about a topic in detail.
EVALUATE	Offer alternative viewpoints about the same topic.
DISCUSS	Give a possibility/consideration about a topic.

HOW ARE YOU GETTING ON?

TAKING NOTES

(Drafting your Response)

TAKING NOTES

DON'T DIVE STRAIGHT IN!

The most important thing to remember when it comes to writing, is to take your time and **PLAN** what you are going to say.

Examiners will know if you have structured your response thoroughly, or just dived head first and written off the top of your head.

Planning is a crucial step for any good writer. There is no wrong or right way to plan; you just need to find a way that you feel comfortable with.

TAKING NOTES FROM WRITTEN TEXT

If you are making notes from a piece of text, you should consider the following:

GENERAL TIPS FOR NOTE TAKING:
1. At the forefront of your mind, should be what the main topics/themes/objectives are.
2. Use bullet points often.
3. Paraphrase key points.
4. Highlight key words and phrases in the text.

TAKING NOTES TO CREATE YOUR OWN WRITING

If you are making notes to write your own piece, you should consider the following:

GENERAL TIPS FOR NOTE TAKING:
1. Consider what you want to say. What is the point you are trying to make? Have a rough idea about what you want to say.
2. Bullet point key points/topics you wish to cover.
3. Consider using spider diagrams to help plan and structure your response.
4. Consider the beginning, middle and end.

Forming a rough plan will really help you to structure your writing, and therefore will allow you to produce better quality written work.

TAKING NOTES

EFFECTIVE NOTE TAKING

1. Keep your notes simple!

- Try not to ramble on.
- Keep your notes on point, focused and short.
- The snappier your notes are, the easier they are to remember.
- Think of keywords and phrases.

2. Know what you want to say!

- Before you begin writing, you will need to know ROUGHLY what it is you want to say.
- What main points do you want to cover?
- What is the purpose of the text?
- Who is going to be reading the text?
- Consider what you want to achieve from your written text.

3. Using spider diagrams

- Spider diagrams help you to keep your notes all on one page.
- At a glance, you are able to clearly see all of your main points/ideas.
- They group points together, which you can then extend even further.

4. Using linear notes

- This is a more detailed way of making notes.
- Your notes will be separated with the use of headings and sub-headings.
- Underline key words and phrases in each section.
- Use abbreviations to shorten your notes down.
- Leave space to add more detail if necessary.
- Bullet points and numbering are great to use under each sub-heading.

DON'T FORGET TO
T.A.P

When writing your notes, you should make sure to consider the following three points:

- **TEXT**
- **AUDIENCE**
- **PURPOSE**

TEXT

Text is just another way of referring to what you are writing. Is the text a magazine article, a newsletter, a diary entry, a story or something else?

Before you begin writing, you first need to plan what you need to include in your writing. Consider the common features of that text. How should you lay out your writing? What language should you use?

For example, a newspaper report would use columns, sub-headings, images and professional language to attract its readers. Whereas a magazine article might be less formal, and would address a very different audience.

AUDIENCE

Who is the text being aimed at? Try and put yourself in the position of the reader? Are they going to understand what you are writing? What would you want to see in your piece of writing?

PURPOSE

Why are you writing the text? Is it to entertain, to inform or to persuade? Or is it a different purpose? Make sure your writing does the job it's supposed to.

Question 1

Circle all of the answers that you should apply to your notes.

ABBREVIATIONS   **LONG PARAGRAPHS**   **BULLET POINTS**

DETAILED QUOTES   **KEY WORDS**   **COLOUR-CODE**

SHORTHAND   **SIMPLE SENTENCES**

Question 2

Why is it a good idea to use colours when note-taking?

Question 3

In effective note-taking, why is it best to use clear, short sentences as opposed to long, wordy sentences? <u>Tick all that apply.</u>

You have plenty of time to write everything down. ☐

You will remember more information. ☐

It will help to formulate some sort of structure when it comes to writing. ☐

You will remember less information. ☐

You won't ramble on. ☐

Question 4

Imagine you are a P.E teacher and you want to encourage more children to play an after-school sport. You decide to write a short speech, which you will use in the next school assembly.

List the key things that you want to include in your speech. Come up with 5 reasons why they should sign up. Marks will be awarded for effective note-taking.

1. _____

_____

_____

2. _____

_____

_____

3. _____

_____

_____

4. _____

_____

_____

5. _____

_____

_____

Question 5

Using your answer from question 4, write the short speech you wish to deliver in the next school assembly.

_____

_____

_____

_____

_____

_____

_____

_____

_____

_____

Question 6

Why is it important to review your notes?

_____

_____

_____

_____

_____

_____

Question 7

Using a spider diagram, make some notes about whether or not schools should ban school uniform.

Question 8

The extract below is entitled *Fitness for Children's Development.* Using bullet points, write down the main points of the extract.

As a society which constantly depicts the importance of healthy lifestyle choices, many people still fail to see the ramifications of their ways.

Eating the right foods and doing plenty of exercise is important for everyone. This is especially true for children, who are at the age of crucial development.

Children need to be eating all of the correct nutrients (minerals and vitamins), which will allow for optimal growth and development. These vitamins and nutritious foods will allow children to feel more energised, more aware, and more motivated. It has been proven that children with a lack of the aforementioned suffer with fatigue, disengagement and a slower rate of development.

Schools are encouraging children to eat healthier. A suggestion has been made for all school children to have school dinners, whereby they will be given a list of nutritious foods, from which they can pick and choose. Options would vary on a daily basis and children would be guaranteed at least one healthy meal during the day.

To ensure children are receiving a healthier lifestyle, parents and schools should focus on variation – varying the choices of food and expanding their diets will ensure that they are receiving good food. Making sure that children receive the right-sized portions, as opposed to dishing up adult-sized portions, will encourage them to not only eat healthy foods, but consume a healthy amount. Alongside eating healthy, children should also be encouraged to exercise.

Exercising doesn't have to be a boring chore for children; this can be fun! Introducing games such as tag, hopscotch and skipping are just a few examples. Ensure your child spends plenty of time outside as opposed to sitting inside. Let them run around until they wear themselves out.

MAIN POINTS

ANSWERS TO TAKING NOTES

Question 1

(ABBREVIATIONS)   LONG PARAGRAPHS   (BULLET POINTS)

DETAILED QUOTES   (KEY WORDS) (COLOUR-CODE)

(SHORTHAND) (SIMPLE SENTENCES)

Question 2

Colour-coding your notes is a great way to link key ideas/words together. That way you can visually see which of your notes work together. This will not only help you to structure your writing more clearly, but it will also allow you to visually memorise your notes more effectively.

Question 3

You have plenty of time to write everything down.	☐
You will remember more information.	✔
It will help to formulate some sort of structure when it comes to writing.	✔
You will remember less information.	☐
You won't ramble on.	✔

Question 4

*Your bullet points could include any idea so long as it ties in with the speech you are preparing.

For example:

- Joining a sporting activity after school will boost your energy and fitness levels.
- Joining a sporting activity will help with your social skills. It will be a great way to make friends.
- Joining a sporting activity will make you feel like you've achieved something.
- You might have a natural talent for a sport, which you could further advance.
- You will be able to represent your school in tournaments, sports days etc.

Question 5

*Your short speech will need to include the points that you listed in question 4. Your answer may be slightly different to the example given below, but this is just to give you an idea of the type of thing you could have written:

How many of you play sports after school? How many of you don't play a sport after school? We have some great sporting activities which may be of interest to you. Now, you might ask: 'Why should I join a sporting activity?' Well, not only is it a great way to exercise and boost your energy levels, but it will also allow you to make friends whilst doing so. You can join with your friends and have an hour or two of fun. Besides, you might have a real talent for it! Sports are a great way for you to feel a sense of achievement, and by representing your school, you will be able to compete in tournaments and competitions, or simply turn up and have some fun!

Question 6

It is important to review your notes just to make sure you have written everything down that you wanted to include in your writing. Also, this will be the time when you can look at your notes again, edit or add information in order to be fully prepared when it comes to writing. Reviewing your notes means that any final adjustments can be made, and you can see whether or not you know exactly what you want to say in your answer.

Question 7

For an answer that is **FOR** keeping school uniforms.

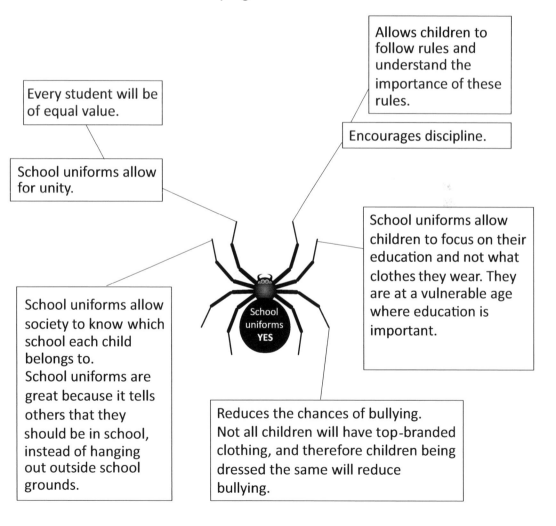

Allows children to follow rules and understand the importance of these rules.

Every student will be of equal value.

Encourages discipline.

School uniforms allow for unity.

School uniforms allow children to focus on their education and not what clothes they wear. They are at a vulnerable age where education is important.

School uniforms allow society to know which school each child belongs to.
School uniforms are great because it tells others that they should be in school, instead of hanging out outside school grounds.

School uniforms YES

Reduces the chances of bullying.
Not all children will have top-branded clothing, and therefore children being dressed the same will reduce bullying.

For an answer that is **AGAINST** keeping school uniforms.

Children are at the age of development. They haven't reached adult life yet, and therefore they should be able to savour their childhood in all manners of speaking.

Encourage students to express themselves individually.

Individualism.

Force children to act older than they are.

Generally, school uniforms are made out of the same material. This material may irritate some children, who are not used to wearing that type of clothing.

School uniforms
NO

School uniforms do detract from learning because students will have to worry whether their tie is the correct length, their skirt is too short or whether their top button is done up.

School uniforms will cost parents more money. Children will already have their own clothes, so they should be able to wear them without having to spend more money on other clothing.

Question 8

- Age of development;
- Optimal growth and development;
- Energised, aware and motivated;
- All school children to have school dinners, whereby they will be given a list of nutritious foods, from which they can pick and choose;
- Should focus on variation;
- Making sure that children receive the right-sized portion;
- Exercising doesn't have to be a boring chore for children; this can be fun!

The above list is just a few examples of the main points made in the extract *'Fitness for Children's Development'*. Make sure you have chosen points that sum up the main points of the text. Remember that this question specifically asks for your answer in bullet point format – use key words and phrases.

STRUCTURING YOUR NOTES

(Drafting your response)

STRUCTURING YOUR NOTES

KEY THINGS TO REMEMBER

When it comes to planning, especially for stories, you want to make sure to draft some key points on a few areas:

The more descriptive you are, the easier your reader will find it to visualise your story.

Characters, narrative, themes and setting are a great way to add some descriptive language to your writing.

Have a go at the below tasks. For the titles, you will need to come up with some descriptive writing for each category.

PRACTICE WRITING 1 - 'THE UNKNOWN'

For this story, your title is 'The Unknown'. What you need to do is fill in the boxes below, in order to come up with a plan for a possible narrative.

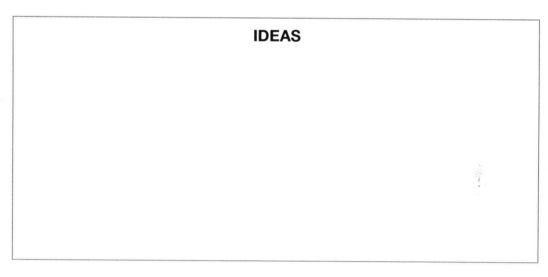

IDEAS

THEMES / MOTIFS

CHARACTERS

SETTING

NARRATIVE

PRACTICE WRITING 2 - 'THE PIRATES AND THE HIDDEN TREASURE CHEST'

For this story, your title is 'The Pirates and the Hidden Treasure Chest'. What you need to do is fill in the boxes below, in order to come up with a plan for a possible narrative.

IDEAS

THEMES / MOTIFS

CHARACTERS

SETTING

NARRATIVE

THE
REVISION
SERIES

BEGINNING, MIDDLE AND END

(Structuring your Writing)

THE IMPORTANCE OF STRUCTURE

STRUCTURING YOUR WRITING

Almost every piece of writing will use a clear and easy-to-follow structure.

Your writing should comprise of these three sections:

- **A BEGINNING**
- **A MIDDLE**
- **AN END**

BEGINNING   **MIDDLE**   **END**

By following this structure, you will ensure that your writing remains clear and focused.

Each of the three components – the beginning, the middle and the end play a vital role in writing. Your writing needs all three of these to prove effective to its reader/audience.

THE BEGINNING

THE BEGINNING – 'INTRODUCTION'

What makes a good introduction? How can we as the writer ensure that our readers stick around to the very end? These questions are exactly the reason why an introduction to a text is so important.

An introduction needs to make your reader want to read on. Below, we have outlined some of the key things that you should consider when writing an introduction:

1.   Hook the reader!

- Introduce the text and set out what your text is going to be about.
- If it is a story, you will want to introduce the main character/s, the setting and tone of the narrative.
- If it's a persuasive text, engage your reader by asking rhetorical questions.
- Understand the topic of the text, who your audience is, and what you want to achieve.

2.   Keep the reader wanting more!

- Your introduction needs to be concise and to the point.
- Do not give too much away in your opening.
- You want the reader to question what they have read and want to read on to find out more.
- Your introduction will need to reflect the type of text you are writing. For example, are you writing a story, a persuasive letter or a newspaper report? Your introduction will use specific features, depending on what type of text you are writing.

THE MIDDLE

THE MIDDLE – 'THE BULK'

The middle of your text is where 'the bulk' of your writing will take place.

This is where everything is going to happen, and will include all of the main points you wish to make.

3.   Maintain reader's interest

- Your writing needs to use powerful literary techniques in order to engage the reader and make them want to read on.
- Consider all of the key points you wish to make and explore how they are relevant/important to the overall text.
- You need to include detailed descriptions.
- Think about TiPToP (see page 74)

4.   Focus on your main points/topics

- If you are writing a story, you need to include obstacles and complications.
- If you are writing a letter, you will need to include the main points you wish to cover. It is best to include a few main points and detail them, as opposed to including lots of points with little detail.
- Remember to use paragraphs for each new point (see page 72)

5.   Make the reader think!

- A good middle will make the reader want to finish the text.
- If it is a story, you need to start resolving the complications in order to end the narrative.
- If it's a letter, what do you want your reader to do/think after reading your text?

THE END

THE END – 'SUMMING UP'

Every piece of writing needs a good ending. Of course, your ending will depend on what type of text you are writing. However, in a generic sense, you need to sum up everything you have written.

> ## 6. Sum up your points/ideas!

- This is where the climax/main points of your text will be resolved.
- This is going to be the last thing that your readers are going to remember. Therefore, you want to make a lasting impression on them.

> ## 7. Make a lasting impression!

- If you are writing a letter, this will use a very formal way of ending. If it's a letter of complaint, your ending sentence should be along the lines of hoping to have an issue resolved. Generally, letters will also end as follows (plus your name):

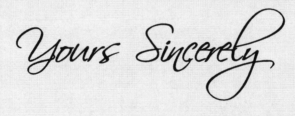

- If you are writing to persuade or argue, then you will want your readers to agree with everything you have said.
- If you are writing a story, your ending will need to sum up everything that has happened, and tie up the overall narrative.
- Your readers should be left feeling satisfied. They should have some idea of what you hoped to achieve, your reasons for it, any implications and a resolution.

Question 1

Which of the following is the best **opening line** for a news article about the issue of global warming?

a) Global warming is an issue that will impact future generations.

b) Have you ever wondered what our world will look like in a few years' time?

c) Sometimes, we are blindsided by our actions and how we treat the world around us.

d) Sarah Parks claims that global warming is on the increase.

Answer [   ]

Question 2

Why is an introduction, a middle, and an end important in story writing? Explain the importance of each and how this helps the reader engage with the story.

_____

_____

_____

_____

_____

_____

_____

_____

_____

_____

Question 3

Write four paragraphs from a short story on a topic of your choice. In your writing you need to include an introduction, two paragraphs from the middle of the story, and a closing paragraph.

<u>Within your writing, you should include ALL of the following:</u>

- Alliteration
- Metaphor
- Personification
- Rhetorical question
- Ellipsis
- Simile

Your writing should be descriptive and entertaining. Think of who you want your target reader to be. <u>Additional paper may be required.</u>

Question 4

Imagine that you are writing an essay arguing for and/or against homework being banned. Using the sentences below, rewrite them in the correct logical order, based on your understanding of how an essay should be structured.

> Give an opposing view about your point, and how people might think differently.

> Outline what your essay is going to consist of, and why it's relevant.

> Insert a reason either for or against.

> Conclude your argument with your opinions, summing up your main points.

> Explain how the alternative point can be challenged. Use this to dismiss their point.

> Back your reason up using examples, evidence and analysis.

1. _____

2. _____

3. _____

4. _____

5. _____

6. _____

ANSWERS TO BEGINNING, MIDDLE AND END

Question 1

A - Have you ever wondered about what our world will look like in a few years' time?

Option A is the best opening line for a news article on global warming because it instantly draws the reader in. The readers are asked a question, which automatically makes the writing interactive. It draws upon ideas about how the world is changing, and introduces the topic that is going to be discussed.

Question 2

An introduction is important as it introduces the narrative that is going to occur. An introduction hooks the reader and sets the scene. Sometimes, it outlines the main character. An introduction needs to leave the reader wanting more.

The middle of a story is where the main events will happen. The story will reach a climax (a turning point). Great writing will make the reader feel all kinds of emotions. This is where you can get really creative with your writing.

The ending of a narrative allows the story to come to a close. The reader needs to feel that the story has been resolved.

Question 3

This answer requires detailed, effective, well-structured writing. Your writing can be on a topic of your choice. Make sure that you have included all of the following:

- Alliteration
- Metaphor
- Personification
- Rhetorical question
- Ellipsis
- Simile

Have someone read through your writing, and pinpoint the above literary techniques. Is your writing entertaining? Is it descriptive? Is it creative? Marks will be awarded for grammar, punctuation and spelling.

Question 4

1. Outline what your essay is going to consist of, and why it's relevant.

2. Insert a reason either for or against.

3. Back your reason up using examples, evidence and analysis.

4. Give an opposing view about your point, and how people might think differently.

5. Explain how the alternative point can be challenged. Use this to dismiss their point.

6. Conclude your argument with your opinions, summing up your main points.

HOW ARE YOU GETTING ON?

PARAGRAPHS AND TIPTOP

(Structuring your Writing)

PARAGRAPHS

WHAT ARE PARAGRAPHS?

Paragraphs consist of groups of sentences which all link to the same topic/theme.

WHAT DO PARAGRAPHS LOOK LIKE

There are two ways you can demonstrate a new paragraph:

1. Leaving a blank line.
2. Indenting the next line.

> Some people use an indent to indicate a new paragraph.
> ⇢ Paragraphs are a great formatting tool which helps to structure your writing.

Make sure the indent spacing is the same throughout the text!

> Other people will leave a line space between each paragraph.
>
> Paragraphs allow your reader to know when they are reading something new.

*Make sure the line gap between each paragraph
is the same throughout the text!*

Whichever paragraph style you use, make sure it is consistent throughout the text.

Now that you've learnt what paragraphs look like, it is time to see when to use a new paragraph!

PARAGRAPHS

WHEN TO USE PARAGRAPHS

Paragraphs are essential when writing. They help to make your writing clearer to read.

You need to use paragraphs in pretty much EVERY literary text you write:

- Stories
- Letters
- Essays
- Articles

Paragraphs should be used to indicate:

- Time
- Place
- Topic
- People

Please see the following page on 'TiPToP' for more information on this.

IF YOU FORGET TO WRITE A NEW PARGRAPH

Sometimes it's easy to forget when to begin a new paragraph. If you do forget to change paragraph in an exam, you should use two forward slash punctuation marks to show you realised your mistake: //

> Some people use an indent to indicate a new paragraph. // Paragraphs are a great formatting tool which helps to structure your writing. // Whilst writing my letter, I included...

TiPToP

DON'T FOGET TO TiPToP!

When formulating your paragraphs, you should think of each paragraph as a stepping stone to the next.

Remember, the main reasons why you should create a new paragraph can be demonstrated by the use of TiPToP!

- **TIME**
- **PLACE**
- **TOPIC**
- **PERSON**

| **Ti** – time | **P** – place |
| **To** – topic | **P** – person |

For every new time period, place, topic/idea, or person speaking, make sure you begin a new paragraph!

PARAGRAPHS

TRY TO LINK YOUR PARAGRAPHS

Your writing will be much clearer and read more coherently if you try to structure your writing so that it flows.

You should have structured your writing using paragraphs. These paragraphs need to flow effortlessly from one to the next.

Using connectives is a great way to make your paragraphs flow.

As a result of...	Alternatively...	So...
In addition...	Although...	Also...
Furthermore...	On the other hand...	Therefore...
Meanwhile...	Finally...	Consequently...

ALL WRITING

No matter what you are writing, you will always need to use paragraphs. Whether you are writing a newspaper article, an email or a letter, you will still need to write in a clear structure.

Remember, structure is important! Paragraphs help make your writing clear and focused.

TIME   **TiPToP**   TOPIC
PLACE   PERSON

Question 1

For the following passage, draw in two forward slash punctuation marks (//) to indicate where a new paragraph should begin.

There were many complaints from students in the aftermath of changes to the school uniform. The changes to the uniform would be coming into effect in the next school year, but new uniform was rolled out to students who needed it at that moment. Any students who were representing the school at events (there weren't many external events at that point in the year) would be required to wear the new uniform. The colour of the school tie had been changed from a deep blue to bright purple, with an emblem at the top. Moreover, the jumpers worn were made brighter, resulting in a clash of colours. Another less controversial change was to rules regarding shoes. Up until this point, the school had allowed dark brown shoes to be worn as well as black shoes; the intention being that it allowed for more freedom in choosing what to wear. However, the school had taken a hard-line stance against brown shoes, only allowing black school shoes to be worn. This would come into effect immediately.

Question 2

What are the four categories which you should remember when working out when to place a new paragraph in your writing?

1. _____

2. _____

3. _____

4. _____

Question 3

Below are six ideas for possible paragraphs. Rearrange these ideas so that they read in the best possible order.

> Serious cases need to come with serious consequences. Suspension or even expulsion should be considered.

> Harsher punishments need to be implemented when it comes to school bullying.

> Bullying has become a serious issue across schools in the UK. The way in which we deal with these issues needs to be reconsidered.

> Socialisation is a key concept regarding young children and adolescents. They are influenced by the people around them.

> Introduce the topic. Explain its importance and what you wish to cover.

> Children are at a vulnerable age. Their peers can make or break who they are at school, and it's important that children socialise in the correct way.

1. _____

_____

2. _____

_____

3. _____

_____

4. _____

_____

5. _____

_____

6. _____

_____

Question 4

Using proper sentences, and 2-3 paragraphs, what are your views on P.E as being a compulsory school subject?

_____

_____

_____

_____

_____

_____

_____

_____

_____

_____

_____

_____

_____

_____

_____

_____

Question 5

Read the following extract, and answer the questions. The following text is an article from a fictional education journal.

The school have opted to introduce the '20th Century Awareness Project', starting with the 'First World War Awareness Programme'. The aim of these two projects is to strengthen younger students' understanding of the events of the 20th Century.

The school's leadership team believed that it was necessary to better teach the history of the 20th Century to all students, particularly the period between 1900-1918. This was due to concerns that younger pupils would not naturally be exposed to the First World War in a sensitive manner, and that depictions of it in popular culture (e.g. film, video-games, television programmes) might not convey the horrors of the war enough, instead choosing to glorify conflict as a whole.

Mrs. Brown, the school's head teacher, claimed that the First World War was 'the most important event in recent history' as it shaped the modern world. To an extent, Mrs. Brown's statement is correct. The League of Nations was founded in 1920 mostly as a response to the events of the First World War, which in turn set a precedent for multinational legislative bodies such as the European Union and the United Nations. Additionally, Germany's defeat in the war and subsequent reparation expenses arguably resulted in the rise of the Nazi party and therefore the Second World War, which would shape the world even further.

Mrs. Brown continued, expressing concern that younger pupils might not be learning about the war outside of school. She argued that if we fail to pass on our understanding of such terrible events to younger generations, people in the future won't know the lessons that we've learnt from history.

a) Sum up what paragraphs three and four are talking about.

_____

_____

_____

_____

b) Why is the fourth paragraph a separate paragraph from paragraph 3?

_____

_____

_____

_____

c) Write a concluding paragraph for this extract, using the points that have been stated in the passage.

_____

_____

_____

_____

_____

_____

_____

_____

_____

_____

_____

_____

_____

_____

ANSWERS TO PARAGRAPHS AND TiPToP

Question 1

There were many complaints from students in the aftermath of changes to the school uniform. The changes to the uniform would be coming into effect in the next school year, but the new uniform was rolled out to students who needed it at that moment. Any students who were representing the school at events (there weren't many external events at that point in the year) would be required to wear the new uniform. **//**The colour of the school tie had been changed from a deep blue to bright purple, with an emblem at the top. Moreover, the jumpers worn were made brighter, resulting in a clash of colours. **//**Another less controversial change was to rules regarding shoes. Up until this point, the school had allowed dark brown shoes to be worn as well as black shoes; the intention being that it allowed for more freedom in choosing what to wear. However, the school had taken a hard-line stance against brown shoes, only allowing black school shoes to be worn. This would come into effect immediately.

Question 2

1. Time
2. Place
3. Topic
4. People

Question 3

1. Introduce the topic. Explain its importance and what you wish to cover.

2. Hasher punishments need to be implemented when it comes to school bullying.

3. Bullying has become a serious issue across schools in the UK. The way in which we deal with these issues needs to be reconsidered.

4. Children are at a vulnerable age. Their peers can make or break who they are at school, and it's important that children socialise in the correct way.

5. Socialisation is a key concept regarding your children and adolescents. They are influenced by the people around them.

6. Serious cases need to come with serious consequences. Suspension or even expulsion should be considered.

Question 4

Your answer needs to focus on your personal views of P.E being a compulsory school subject.

You could focus on some of the following points:

- Promote active lifestyle.

- Teaches children how to follow discipline, rules and structure.

- Physical activity helps to reduce stress levels.

- P.E. lessons promote social interaction.

- The opportunity to learn a new sport and continue their development and potential.

Remember, when beginning a new point, you need to begin a new paragraph. Your sentences should be written formally, well punctuated and express your views in a clear and concise manner.

Have a friend, parent or teacher look over your response to see whether you are structuring your writing correctly.

Question 5

a) Paragraph three shows the concerns and opinions from the head teacher's point of view. She claims that students need to learn more about the First World War due to the topic being a significant event in English history. Students need to be made aware about culture and history, and how this has affected them.

b) Paragraph four is separate from paragraph three because it is addressing a different point. Although the two paragraphs are concerned with the same person (Mrs. Brown), she changes focus in each paragraph. The third paragraph talks about the importance of the League of Nations and the effect this had on history, whereas paragraph four expresses her actual concerns and that younger generations need to be made aware of historical contexts.

c) *Your concluding paragraph needs to sum up the main points of the extract. Your summary could be along the lines of the following:*

It is evident that past events shape future generations. Therefore, these generations need to be taught about the importance of such events, such as the First World War. Schools have introduced new programmes to emphasise the importance of these events. This will help to increase student's awareness and historical knowledge, and therefore contribute to the cause of creating well-rounded, educated citizens.

HOW ARE YOU GETTING ON?

THE
REVISION
SERIES

ESSAY WRITING

(Writing with a Purpose)

ESSAY WRITING

Essays are a great way to structure your writing.

Essays are a form of writing which allow you to answer a question.

WHAT ALL GOOD ESSAYS NEED

All good essays need a clear and focused structure. You can achieve this by creating an introduction, a middle and an end.

INTRODUCTION

- Outline what direction your essay is going to take.
- You could include a hypothesis.
- Use keywords from the question.
- 2-3 sentences is sufficient for an introduction.
- The reader should be able to read your introduction and conclusion, and know what your essay is about.

MAIN BODY

- Answer the question by making 3-4 points.
- Support these points with examples, quotes and analysis.
- Make sure you keep referring to the question.
- 3-4 paragraphs is sufficient for an essay.
- Analyse and explain key points, their relevance and your opinions.

CONCLUSION

- Summarise the key points you've made and how they are important/relevant.
- DO NOT introduce any new points in the conclusion.
- Make sure you write a sentence referring to the question.
- The reader should be able to read your introduction and conclusion, and know what your essay is about.

ESSAY WRITING

On the next few pages, I have created a template which you can use and redraw to help you when it comes to structuring your essays. I've also provided a sample essay, and highlighted key points throughout the essay.

As well as structure, essays also need to flow, use effective language, use the correct tone, and of course, answer the question.

ESSAY FEATURES	EXPLANATION
Language	Consider what language is best. For essays, formal and technical language is great. Use long fancy words only if you know the meaning of them.
Tone and style	You need to set the tone. Is it a serious or light-hearted essay? Your language should reflect this.
Paragraphing	Use a paragraph for each new point. Your introduction and conclusion will form paragraphs, and then you'll have 3 or 4 paragraphs for your main body.
Literary techniques	Avoid repetition. Rhetorical questions are great to interact your reader. Consider what techniques you can use to enhance your writing (metaphors, personification etc.)

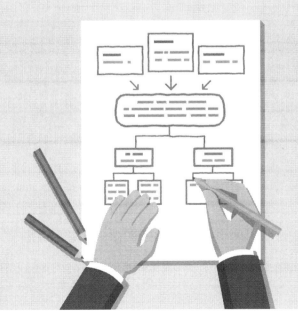

ESSAY WRITING

KEY WORDS AND PHRASES

For each section of your essay, I have provided some key words and phrases that you could use for each part of your essay.

INTRODUCTORY WORDS
In this essay
We are introduced to
Within this essay
I am going to

OPINIONATED WORDS
I believe
I think
I am convinced
My opinion
My point of view
I feel
It seems that

TRANSITION WORDS
First/second/third
Consequently
Although
Equally important
In addition
Obviously
Furthermore
Additionally

CONCLUSION WORDS
In conclusion
Finally
In summary
Overall
We can see that

QUESTION

INTRODUCTION

MAIN BODY 1

MAIN BODY 2

MAIN BODY 3

IMPORTANT QUOTES / KEYWORDS

CONCLUSION

Should animal testing be banned?

Title

Intro. It's short, concise and uses keywords from the question.

Animal testing has become a hugely debated topic as to whether or not it is morally right. Within this essay, I am going to focus on the reasons why animal testing should be banned, and how societal values should reconsider animal testing.

    Primarily, you could argue that animal testing is extremely inhumane. Without going into graphic detail, there are numerous examples of how testing human medicines and cosmetics on animals has resulted in unimaginable pain and suffering for the animals themselves. Testing methods include putting bleach in animals' eyes, forcing them to take pills which result in cardiac arrest or cause allergic reactions, putting makeup on animals etc.

Main Body 1. This introduces your first point. Supported with examples to strengthen point.

    From a moral standpoint, we would be vehemently opposed to anyone who forced other human beings to take part in this, and therefore we shouldn't inflict it on animals. The testing that is performed on animals could easily be performed on human volunteers, we are just scared of the effects that they will have and the media firestorm that would result if one of the volunteers died. Although human testing does take place, the testing is done under humane conditions where the volunteers are not treated anywhere near as badly as animal test subjects.

Main Body 2. Second main point. Comparing animals to humans.

    Animals have rights and feelings and should be treated with respect. This is especially true for cosmetic products. While there is some justification for medical testing, there is absolutely no reason to harm animals in the name of makeup or vanity. Furthermore, animal testing is extremely unreliable. The effect that a product has on an animal is not always indicative of the effect that it will have on a human being.

Main Body 3. Point about morals. This uses effects to show implications.

    However, enormous medical advances have been made possible by animal testing. Without animal testing, modern medicine would simply not be where it is today. By testing on animals we have been able to save billions of lives, and develop essential vaccines which save children. If you were in a hospital, threatened with a life-saving illness, you wouldn't reject medication that could save you based on the fact that it had been tested on animals first.

Counter argument 1. Using a counter argument shows you have considered both sides of the argument.

    Likewise, cosmetic products play an extremely important role in society. In particular, they dramatically increase the self-confidence of women, who can then go out and impact on our world in a much bigger way.

Counter argument 2. Showing your knowledge and understanding about the topic.

    Fundamentally, animal testing has failed to reach a solution on a huge number of medical issues for human beings. Despite decades of trying to cure the likes of Alzheimer's disease, diabetes, aids and cancer, using animals as test subjects, we still do not have a reliable cure. We have been curing cancer in mice for years now, but are still no closer to doing the same for humans. We are wasting time and money, and inflicting unimaginable suffering on innocent animals.

Dismissal. Dismissing the counter arguments.

    Although there are advantages and disadvantages to animal testing, the fact remains that animals are used to test products is immoral. Animals have done nothing wrong to deserve to be treated the way they are during animal testing. I believe animals have just as much right as humans, and we are not subjected to this kind of testing, so why should they?

Conclusion. Sums up the overall argument. Shares your opinions.

Question 1

Should prisoners be allowed to vote?

Question 2

Should schools be banned from serving junk food?

ANSWERS TO ESSAY WRITING

Question 1

This question requires you to give your opinion on whether you believe that prisoners should be allowed to vote. This is a controversial issue in a number of countries, not least in the UK, where prisoners are unable to do so. You will need to weigh up all of the pros and cons before coming to a clear conclusion, based on logic, law and reasoning. Your argument could include a discussion on whether prisoners as a whole should be unable to vote, or whether this privilege should extend only to those who have or haven't committed certain crimes.

Introduction. In your introduction, you should clearly lay out your opinion on whether you believe that prisoners should be allowed to vote. You could introduce the current state of the law, which prevents prisoners from voting, and give some explanation on the controversy surrounding the issue. You could use brief law based examples to typify your point, before listing any assumptions or assertions that you expect to make in your essay.

For. In order to argue for prisoners being allowed to vote, there are a number of points that you could make:

- Firstly, you could argue that not allowing prisoners to vote is a violation of human rights. The reality is that these people have been imprisoned for two reasons a) to protect the public and b) as part of a rehabilitation service. Denying prisoners the right to vote does not protect the public, and directly contradicts the latter. Prisoners are still members of society and citizens of the nation, and therefore have the right to civil liberties.

- In line with the above point, we live in a democratic society. This is a society which takes pride in the participation of all its people in the political process; regardless of how much money they have, their gender, their sexual orientation or class. By denying prisoners the right to represent themselves on a political level, we are contradicting the democracy that Western civilisation uses as its trump card.

- You could argue that keeping prisoners as part of the democratic process will increase their chances of adjusting back into civilian life. By not allowing them to vote, you are disenfranchising prisoners from society, reducing their sense of self-worth and increasing their bitterness towards those who have imprisoned them in the first place.

- You could also argue that certain prisoners should be allowed to vote, but not others. Murderers or serial killers for example, have committed 'the ultimate crime' and therefore should not be given a voice. However, those who have committed minor crimes should not be denied a political voice.

Against. In order to argue against giving prisoners the right to vote, there are a number of points you could make:

- Firstly, you could argue that prisoners have forfeited their role as members of our society, by refusing to respect the rules in which we follow. If they cannot keep to the laws, in particular if they have committed murder, they don't deserve the right to decide who leads and governs us. Their refusal to act responsibly in a democratic system means that their views and needs should not be represented by the system. The right to vote should be granted to trusted members of society, not those who have proved that they can't be trusted.

- Secondly, you could argue that denying prisoners the right to vote represents an excellent form of deterrent. Banning prisoners from voting is a fundamental part of the prison package, which separates offenders from innocent people. While banning prisoners from voting does not work as a deterrent on its own; as part of a set of regulations it combines to show society's disapproval of those who break our established rules, and lays down a strong marker.

- In line with the above, you could argue that rehabilitating offenders is not about mollycoddling them. It is about making them realise the severity of their actions, by isolating them from well-behaved members of society. Only once prisoners have realised the consequences of their actions, i.e. not being able to vote, can they begin the path to true rehabilitation.

- You could argue against only giving certain prisoners a vote, by stating that this would cause enormous issues. For example, how would you draw the line between a serial killer and someone who has killed out of self-defence, or even someone who has been wrongly convicted? If you give one prisoner the vote, this needs to apply to everyone, or you risk causing a serious imbalance.

Counter. In order to counter the above, you could argue that by denying prisoners their civil liberties, we are acting in a manner that is no better than the prisoners themselves. Yes prison is meant to rehabilitate offenders, but part of rehabilitation means that we need to set an example to the offenders. Taking away their civil rights reduces them to nothing, and will only make them angrier and more disenfranchised in the long run.

Conclusion. In your conclusion, you should clearly state your view on whether prisoners should be allowed to vote. You should include the pros and cons of each side of the argument, and back up your answer with logical and sustained reasoning from your essay, to come to a fair summary on the issue.

Question 2

This question requires you to give your opinion on whether you believe that schools should be allowed to serve their pupils 'junk food'. In your essay, you should clearly define what you infer by the term 'junk food', the pros and cons of banning it from schools and what you believe should be done about this. You should make reference to issues such as childhood obesity, school dinners, vending machines and packed lunches.

Introduction. In the introduction to your essay, you should clearly state your view on whether you believe that schools should be banned from serving junk food. You could define what is meant by the term 'junk food', make brief reference to issues such as obesity and school dinners, before listing some of the assertions and assumptions that you expect to make in your essay.

For. In order to argue for schools being banned from serving junk food, there are a number of points that you could make:

- Primarily, you could argue that Britain has a growing obesity problem. It is our responsibility to tackle this, and it starts with children. Numerous studies have shown that if children are introduced to bad lifestyle habits at an early age, these habits will continue with them as they get older, and have a negative impact upon their life. The earlier we deal with obesity, the lesser the chance of us having obese adults.

- Next, you could point out that it is down to schools to set a good example for children. Children spend the vast proportion of their adolescent lives in school, with days going on for 6 hours or more. The school curriculum lectures children in topics such as health, sex and relationships. How can schools actively preach these subjects when they are handing out junk food to their pupils?

- You could also point out that in some schools, school dinner is not free. Parents pay a significant fee for these dinners, so therefore it is extremely unjust for schools to then serve their children poor quality meals. If parents are paying, they should expect their children to eat nutritious and healthy food.

- Finally, you could point out that there is a growing bevy of evidence which links healthy school dinners with academic performance. Eating healthily and staying fit results in having an improved memory and concentration span, and leads to a more motivated outlook. Studies have linked the consumption of three or more junk based meals in a week with a noticeable drop in literacy and numeracy skills.

Against. In order to argue against schools being banned from serving school dinners, there are a number of points that you could make:

- Firstly, you could argue that the responsibility of serving healthy meals should not be placed on schools. School is a place for children to learn. If parents want their children to be healthy, then they should provide them with a healthy packed lunch, ensure that they eat nutritious dinners and take them on brisk walks/exercise. Schools are already financially and operationally overburdened by the budget cuts, and taking on more students than ever before. By asking them to incorporate healthy dinners into their itinerary, you are placing yet another demand upon a struggling system.

- Secondly, you could argue that forcing children to eat healthily would violate their right to freedom of choice. We live in a democratic society, where people can make their own decisions. Telling children that they can't eat this or that is the wrong way to go about dealing with obesity. Instead, schools should place more emphasis on teaching pupils the importance of a healthy lifestyle, rather than forcing it on them.

- Thirdly, you could point out that in actual fact, administering behavioural changes in school is not an accurate indication of how children will behave outside of it. 6 hours in school every day is a long time, but it doesn't account for the whole day. The availability of junk food outside of school is extremely prominent, and therefore providing healthy meals in schools is not a way of preventing children from eating badly outside of them. Research has shown that children will happily go outside of school to find their favourite junk food, rather than eating healthy meals inside of it.

Counter. You could counter the above by arguing that schools are not forcing children to eat their healthy meals, by banning junk food. They are simply putting a system in place where it is harder for children to purchase these unhealthy meals. Combined with teaching healthy values, this more than fulfils the schools' quota of responsibility, and therefore is something we should be looking into implementing.

Conclusion. In your conclusion, you should clearly state your view on whether schools should be allowed to serve junk food to their pupils, and the pros and cons of each side of the argument. You should back your answer up with logical and sustained reasoning, and use the main points from your essay to come to a fair summary on the issue.

HOW ARE YOU GETTING ON?

STORY WRITING

(Writing with a Purpose)

STORY WRITING

Story writing is a great way for you to get creative.

USE A PLAN

All great stories start with a simple idea. This idea is then expanded upon, using descriptions, imagery and language.

Plans are a great way to structure what you want to say. For more information on how to plan, please read the chapter on planning (see page 35).

THE IMPORTANCE OF ORIGINALITY

Every good story comes from a simple idea. However, that idea needs to demonstrate some originality. What is going to make your story different from everyone else's?

Take an idea and make it your own; add a twist or unusual event which makes it different from stories that have already been told.

STORY WRITING

TELLING A STORY

When you are telling a story, it is important to pay particular attention to the following:

- Language
- Structure
- Tone
- Characters / Characterisation
- Setting
- Narrative
- Audience

KEEPING YOUR READER ENGAGED

Right from the offset, your story needs to be exciting. The beginning of your story needs to be able to keep the reader's attention.

Nobody will want to keep reading if the story starts out as boring, and doesn't improve.

STRUCTURING YOUR WRITING

With every great story, comes a well-thought out structure of events.

The way in which a story pans out has carefully been crafted by the author. The author wants to hook you in right from the start; they want to use action and events to keep you thoroughly entertained; and they want an ending that is original and fitting to the rest of the narrative.

That is why an introduction, a middle and an end are extremely important!

STORY WRITING

To better your writing, you will need to undergo practice; the more practice you do, the better your writing will become.

Remember, writing is all about finding your voice!

In this chapter, I am going to talk you through how to create successful stories, and provide you with some useful tips to improve your writing ability.

STRUCTURING YOUR STORY

The first thing you need to understand is that the structure of your story is important. It allows the reader to be engaged instantly, and be kept excited until the very end.

Every story has a beginning, middle and end:

BEGINNING

- Introducing your reader to your style of writing.
- Setting up the scene and introducing the main characters.
- Creating a 'situation' or 'problem' right at the beginning will make sure that your reader is instantly 'hooked'.
- You need to grab the reader's attention. Make it thrilling. Make it fast-paced. Make the reader want to continue reading.
- Don't give away all of the key details at the beginning. Provide your readers with enough information, so that they will want to continue reading on to find out more.

MIDDLE

- This is where the bulk of your story will take place.
- You need to hold the reader's attention by maintaining a plotline that is interesting, and will push the reader to finish the story.
- Develop obstacles and complications which the characters need to solve.
- Although there might be a few complications, your story should reach a CLIMAX or turning point.
- There is a massive situation which the main character has to try and resolve.
- A good middle will allow the reader to wonder how the story will end.

END

- This is where the climax or turning point of your story will become resolved.
- Your main character/s will have learnt a lesson, or come to terms with the events that have happened.
- A good ending will allow the reader to continue thinking about the story, even after finishing reading it.

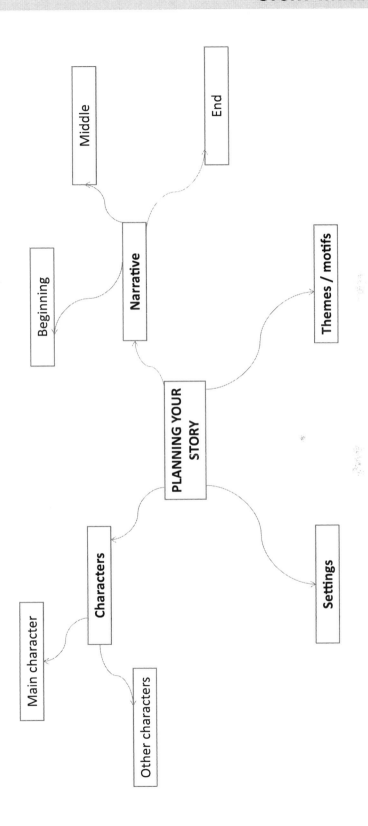

PRACTICE WRITING - 'IN THE DEEP'

For this story, your title is 'IN THE DEEP'. What you need to do is fill in the boxes below, in order to come up with a plan for a possible narrative.

This is a great way to improve your writing skills. Remember, planning your answer will allow your writing to flow better.

IDEAS

THEMES / MOTIFS

CHARACTERS

SETTINGS

NARRATIVE

Question 1

Write an opening paragraph for a horror story.

_____

_____

_____

_____

_____

_____

_____

_____

_____

_____

_____

_____

_____

_____

_____

_____

_____

Question 2

For each of the below genres, write the end paragraph for an original story. Use your imagination and ensure that your ending paragraph is engaging. <u>Additional paper will be required.</u>

Fairy tale	Sci-fi	Horror
Crime	Adventure	Romance

Question 3

Change the following simple sentences into descriptive sentences. <u>Your sentence should be no longer than two or three lines.</u>

a) There was a knock at the door but there was no one there.

_____

_____

b) The man walked into the woods.

_____

_____

c) A little girl lost her mum in the supermarket.

_____

_____

d) The volcano erupted and civilians started running.

_____

_____

Question 4

Write a short story, containing three or four paragraphs about a fear you have. <u>This can be true or completely fictional.</u>

You must consider the following:

- Your story should be written in 1st person;
- Literary techniques such as metaphors and similes should be used where appropriate;
- It should be aimed at a teenage audience;
- Focus on imagery and description;
- Grammar, punctuation and spelling will be assessed.

PLAN:

SHORT STORY:

ANSWERS TO STORY WRITING

Question 1

This needs to draw the reader in immediately. Remember, a horror story needs to be both terrifying and exhilarating.

When writing, consider the following:

- How are you going to introduce the setting?
- What language are you going to use?
- Similes and metaphors are great for horror writing.
- Descriptive writing will allow you to set the tone of the scene.
- Introduce a main character.
- Focus on imagery.
- Focus on senses – taste, touch, sight, sound, smell.

For example:

A horrifying cry echoed through the crisp, night air. My heart leapt out of my chest. Every which way looked the same. I was surrounded, trapped by tall trees; and as I stood in the middle of the forest, I began to feel a terrifying sense of defeat.

I tried to catch my breath. I thought about running. But where to? I was totally lost. Leaves and twigs crunched beneath my toes. The forest was a maze, and I would be trapped here forever and ever, lost for all time; my bones slowly becoming one with the earth and trees and sky...

Footsteps.

Try and create an opening which is fitting to a horror narrative. Think about what type of feelings and setting you wish to convey.

Question 2

For each paragraph, you need to demonstrate the different style narratives. Ensure that your writing is relevant to the genre you are writing in. For example, a fairy tale and romance ending generally consists of a happy ever after, a crime story could end with death and/or destruction.

The narrative that you choose needs to be relevant. Whilst your choice of narrative does not matter, you need to make sure that a) it fits in with the genre, b) you use the correct language, c) consider the audience/reader, and d) emphasise the key features of each genre.

Question 3

Your answers will most likely be different to these. The examples below are showing you how you can effectively add description to your writing.

a) Suddenly, there was a slow knock at the door. The hinges creaked. Yet... there was no one there.

b) The hairy, dreary-eyed man, walked into the cordoned-off woods, suspiciously.

c) The little girl, who was wearing a blue and white pleated uniform, turned back to notice that she had lost in her mum in the busy supermarket.

d) The largest active volcano fiercely erupted and terrified civilians started running in every direction.

Question 4

Your story will be based on fears. This could be from personal feelings or made-up. You will be awarded marks for focusing on each of the bullet points listed in the question.

Ensure that you have someone read through your short story. Ask them to give you feedback – both positive and improvements. This will help you to improve your writing skills.

Remember to focus on the following points:

- _Your story should be written in 1st person;_
- _Literary techniques such as metaphors and similes should be used where appropriate;_
- _It should be aimed at a teenage audience;_
- _Focus on imagery and description;_
- _Grammar, punctuation and spelling will be assessed._

HOW ARE YOU GETTING ON?

THE
REVISION
SERIES

ARGUE, PERSUADE AND ADVISE

(Writing with a Purpose)

ARGUE

When it comes to writing, sometimes you will be required to write in a particular *format*.

WRITING TO ARGUE

Writing to argue is a piece of writing where you argue a particular point.

Arguments in writing are very different from verbal arguments. In verbal arguments, you can be passionate and say what you want. Whereas, in writing, you still need to remain structured and formal.

GAPS	EXPLANATION
G – genre	What kind of writing document are you writing? (Letters, article, speech, story). Whatever form of writing you use, you will need to adhere to the conventions.
A – audience	Who is your targeted audience? Consider age group and what kind of language and style you need to use in order to appeal to your reader.
P – purpose	For argument texts, you need to change the minds of your readers. The keyword to remember is **influence**.
S – style	Informal vs. formal. Again, this will depend on your audience.

Things to consider:

- Consider both views of the argument;
- You need to write a rational well-balanced argument using descriptions and explanations;
- Emphasise your points by making them sound really good.
- Facts and statistics are great to use in writing;
- Dismiss opposing views.

PERSUADE

WRITING TO PERSUADE

Writing to persuade uses similar techniques as writing to argue. Both of these styles of writing require you to influence your reader.

Generally, when writing to persuade, you don't have to offer alternative viewpoints; you simply have to present your own ideas.

FOR EXAMPLE:

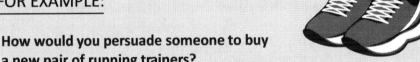

How would you persuade someone to buy a new pair of running trainers?

- You would need to work out who your audience is;
- You would need to use emotive language to appeal to the reader;
- You would need to use evidence and support your reasoning (i.e. comfort, price, durable, high quality etc.);
- You would need to be positive in your way of writing;
- You would need to be personal;
- Language is your ammunition to sell the product;
- Exaggerate your points but DO NOT lie;
- Compare it to your competitors and say how yours is better.

PLAY ON YOUR READER'S EMOTIONS

A great piece of persuasive writing will use expressive language to emphasise key points and persuade the reader/audience to buy, or consider something.

You need to exert yourself and make your writing sound impressive! Repeat things, use questions and statistics, be personal and use feelings to get your viewpoints across!

ADVISE

WRITING TO ADVISE

If you are asked to write a text to advise on something, this basically means that you need to offer your opinion and ideas.

| ADVISE | = | ADVICE | = | HELP |

This is a much gentler way of writing as opposed to written arguments or persuasive texts.

FOR EXAMPLE:

A school is trying to raise money for a charity close to their hearts. You are asked to advise the children on ideas about fundraising, and what needs to be done.

- Offer your personal opinions. You don't have to give definitive reasons, but friendly suggestions and advice.
- Instead of using words like "should" or "will", you should use words like "could" or "might". This demonstrates that you are simply offering help.
- Focus on an idea you could use (i.e. car washes, bake sales etc.) and show how you could run the event smoothly.
- You can consider more than one option. Advising someone means offering ideas and opinions.

Your writing should be gentle, soft and friendly. You are NOT making commands; instead you are offering suggestions.

Question 1

Read the following sentences and decide whether they are written to **advise**, **persuade** or **argue**. Circle the correct answer.

a) A speech about possible activities you can take up during the summer holidays.

    ADVISE   **PERSUADE**   **ARGUE**

b) An email that highlights the key features of a holiday resort in Spain.

    ADVISE   **PERSUADE**   **ARGUE**

c) An essay about the advantages and disadvantages of social networking.

    ADVISE   **PERSUADE**   **ARGUE**

d) A speech about why you should elect a person for president.

    ADVISE   **PERSUADE**   **ARGUE**

Question 2

Write the definition of a persuasive text, using examples to help support your answer.

_____

_____

_____

_____

_____

_____

_____

_____

_____

Question 3

Write two paragraphs to advise someone on how to stay safe on social network sites.

_____

_____

_____

_____

_____

_____

_____

_____

_____

Question 4

Describe how the language would differ between a written piece to argue, and a written piece to persuade.

_____

_____

_____

_____

_____

_____

_____

_____

_____

Question 5

Write a letter to Mr Watson, the school's head teacher, to convince him that a trip to the London Museum would be beneficial for students.

<u>When writing this letter, consider the following:</u>

- You are writing from the perspective of a child who attends that school;
- Use persuasive language to get your points across;
- Pay particular attention to grammar, punctuation and spelling;
- Use at least one rhetorical question;
- Use three valid points to support your writing.

Dear Mr Watson,

Question 6

Below is a table which you need to fill in. For each style of writing, you should include at least 3 key features of the style, and an example text.

	KEY FEATURES	EXAMPLE
ADVISE		
PERSUADE		
ARGUE		

ANSWERS TO ARGUE, PERSUADE AND ADVISE

Question 1

a) A speech about possible activities you can take up during the summer holidays.

ADVISE（circled）　　　　**PERSUADE**　　　　**ARGUE**

b) An email that highlights the key features of a holiday resort in Spain.

ADVISE　　　　**PERSUADE**（circled）　　　　**ARGUE**

c) An essay about the advantages and disadvantages of social networking.

ADVISE　　　　**PERSUADE**　　　　**ARGUE**（circled）

d) A speech about why you should elect a person for president.

ADVISE　　　　**PERSUADE**（circled）　　　　**ARGUE**

Question 2

Persuasive texts are used to help people see things from your point of view. Persuasive writing makes readers think about something, often in relation to buying a new product. Magazines, TV adverts and brochures often use persuasive writing to appeal to their readers/audience and persuade them to buy or consider something.

Question 3

*Your paragraphs should focus on alternative ways that people can stay safe on social networking sites. Remember, to advise someone is to offer different opinions, you are not forcing them to do something.

<u>For example:</u>

- Advise people to stay safe by suggesting that they change their settings to private. This will ensure that only their friends will be able to view their profiles.
- Don't add or interact with strangers.
- Don't give in to peer pressure.
- Ensure your passwords are strong and are regularly updated. This will prevent people from hacking into your account.
- Be careful about what you post online. Future employees might use your social networking sites to determine whether you are suitable for a job. Things you post online can come back to haunt you.
- Remember that things you post online can never be properly removed from the internet.

Your two paragraphs will include at least one main point in each. These points will need to be expanded, using examples and analysis to support why that point is significant. Remember, grammar, punctuation and spelling are considered in your writing.

Question 4

A piece that is written to argue is much more direct and forceful than a persuasive text. Persuasive texts rely on emotive and personal language to appeal to the reader. Writing to argue should use rational and well-balanced arguments which should not rely on emotions or passion. Argumentative texts need to be quite authoritative in how they come across to the reader; the author needs to use language that is technical, to the point and relatively formal.

Question 5

Your writing for this answer requires you to understand the structure and content of a letter. Remember to use paragraphs in your work to make your writing clear and focused.

Remember to pay attention to the following:

- You are writing from the perspective of a child who attends that school;
- Use persuasive language to get your points across;
- Pay particular attention to grammar, punctuation and spelling;
- Use at least one rhetorical question;
- Use three valid points to support your writing.

Get a parent or teacher to read your letter and see how well your writing matches the requirements of a formal letter.

Question 6

	KEY FEATURES	EXAMPLE
ADVISE	• Friendly language • Offer opinions • Make recommendations	• How to boil an egg • How to stay safe online • How to adapt to a new school
PERSUADE	• Emotive language • Adjectives • Be personal	• An advert for a new brand of clothes • A billboard for banning smoking • A radio advert for a new album
ARGUE	• Forceful language • Strong opinions • Present views from both sides	• For or against no smoking ban • Debate about school uniforms • Is animal testing moral?

HOW ARE YOU GETTING ON?

THE
REVISION
SERIES

EXPLAIN, INFORM AND DESCRIBE

(Writing with a Purpose)

EXPLAIN, INFORM AND DESCRIBE

WRITING TO EXPLAIN

EXPLAIN	**=**	**EXPLANATION**

When you are writing to explain, you will provide information that is factual, and provide details about something.

FOR EXAMPLE:

Explain the importance of exercise.

* For this question, you need to provide facts about why exercise is important.
* You will do this by providing reasons, examples and analysis to justify your response.

Useful techniques in explanative writing:

* Generally written in third person;
* Written in past or present tense;
* Use connectives to compare;
* Clear, factual language;
* Use examples and evidence to support your writing.

EXPLAIN, INFORM AND DESCRIBE

WRITING TO INFORM

> **INFORM** = **INFORMATION**

When you are writing to inform, you would provide the basic facts. The main difference between informing and explaining, is that explanations require more detail.

FOR EXAMPLE:

Inform the students about school uniform policies.

- Basic, straightforward language to convey the key information about school uniform policies.
- Give information about what the school uniform policies are, and why they're important.

Useful techniques in informative writing:

- Clear, factual informal;
- Information should be impersonal;
- Provide facts through examples and statistics;
- Consider what, where, when, how and why;
- Language should reflect the mood and genre of the text.

EXPLAIN, INFORM AND DESCRIBE

WRITING TO DESCRIBE

DESCRIBE	**=**	DESCRIPTION

Generally, writing to describe will draw upon emotions and feelings.

FOR EXAMPLE:

Describe a setting by the lake.

- Describe the lake using adjectives and emotive language.
- Consider how the lake makes you feel. Draw upon your senses – sight, sound, smell, taste, touch.

Useful techniques in descriptive writing:

- Strong use of adjectives;
- Use of similes, metaphors, personification, pathetic fallacy, hyperbole etc.;
- Senses – sight, sound, touch, taste, smell;
- Emotive language – create an emotional response;
- Allow your readers to visualise characters and settings.

Question 1

Give a definition of each *type* of text, and give an example of a text used to inform, explain and describe.

EXPLANATIVE TEXTS

_____

_____

_____

EXAMPLE

_____

_____

INFORMING TEXTS

_____

_____

_____

EXAMPLE

_____

_____

DESCRIBING TEXTS

_____

_____

_____

EXAMPLE

_____

_____

The Water Cycle by How2Become.

THE WATER CYCLE – PROCESS

On earth, water is constantly being **recycled**. This process is known as **the water cycle**, which supplies us with all the water we use.

STEP 1

Water gets evaporated from the earth, into the air.

- The sun heats up the water on Earth and causes it to turn from a liquid to water vapour (a gas). You cannot see the water rising from the ground into the air.

- Water is evaporated from rainwater on the ground, as well as from lakes, rivers and ponds.

STEP 2

The water vapour condenses and forms clouds.

- After the water is in the air, the water vapour cools down and turns into tiny water droplets. These droplets form a cloud.

STEP 3

Rain begins to fall.

- Clouds become heavy, and these tiny water droplets fall back to earth. This is either in the form of rain, sleet or snow.

STEP 4

Water returns to the sea.

- Rain water lays on the ground and is collected in lakes and rivers, and transports it back to the sea. The process then starts all over again.

Question 2

What type of non-fiction text is this? Tick **one**.

Instruction text

Persuasive text

Discussion text

Explanation text

How do you know this?

_____

_____

Question 3

Describe your perfect day out.

_____

_____

_____

_____

_____

_____

_____

_____

_____

_____

_____

Question 4

Below are two extracts. Read the extracts and work out whether the extract is used to inform, explain or persuade.

> My favourite subject at school is P.E. Not only do I get to play sports I love, but I also get to try out new sports. This is a great way for you to keep fit, decrease your stress levels, and build confidence in social environments. My favourite sport is running. Long distance running is what I am best at; I am able to pace myself at a steady rhythm and keep my breathing under control.

INFORM   **EXPLAIN**   **PERSUADE**

How do you know?

_____

_____

_____

_____

> Students who are about to pick their GCSEs, face a difficult decision. I recommend studying P.E. I recommend that, for your P.E lessons, you invest in a good pair of trainers. This will allow you to move about with ease and control. Comfort is also another thing to take into consideration. A good pair of trainers will prevent injuries and improve your posture.

INFORM   **EXPLAIN**   **PERSUADE**

How do you know?

_____

_____

_____

_____

Question 5

WHAT IS A VOLCANO?

The origin of the word volcano comes from the word 'Vulcan' – a god of fire in Roman Mythology.

Most volcanoes are mountains and found in the Pacific Ocean. Magma and poisonous gases build up before exploding through the Earth's surface.

A volcano is a type of landform that opens downwards to a pool of molten rock (magma).

HOW ARE VOLCANOES FORMED?

The Earth has three layers – the crust (at the top), the mantle (the middle), and the core (the centre).

The formation of volcanoes is quite simple. When magma, from below the Earth's upper mantle, works its way to the surface, this creates an eruption.

DIFFERENT STAGES OF VOLCANOES

There are three main categories which define what kind of volcano it is – active, dormant and extinct.

An active volcano is a volcano that is or has erupted recently, and is likely to erupt again.

A dormant volcano is a volcano that has not erupted recently, but is likely to erupt.

An extinct volcano is a volcano that has not erupted and is not expected to erupt.

WHY DO VOLCANOES ERUPT?

Volcanoes erupt due to the friction between the plates of the Earth's crust. These 'tectonic plates' fit together like a jigsaw puzzle, and when these plates move, it causes the volcano to erupt.

Volcanoes are also suggested to trigger other natural disasters such as earthquakes, flooding, mud flows, rock falls and tsunamis.

EFFECTS OF VOLCANOES

Eruptions of volcanoes have long-lasting effects on both humans and the environment.

Some of the consequences following a volcano eruption include:

- Destroyed buildings;
- Destroyed habitats and landscapes;
- People becoming homeless;
- People being killed or seriously injured;
- Ash covering plants, making them inedible;
- Poisonous gases killing people and animals;
- Dark skies, strong winds and heavy rain may follow.

THE MAUNA LOA

The Mauna Loa (meaning Long Mountain) is the largest active shield volcano in the world. That means it's built almost entirely of fluid magma flows.

This volcano is one of five that forms the Island of Hawaii in the Pacific Ocean.

Having erupted over 33 times since 1843, the Mauna Loa is taller than Mount Everest if measured from its base below sea level to its summit.

What type of literary text is this? Circle **one**.

INSTRUCTION   **EXPLANATION**   **PERSUASION**   **INFORMATIVE**

Explain how you know this.

_____

_____

_____

_____

Question 6

Write a letter explaining the reasons why schools should provide free hot, healthy school meals.

_____

_____

_____

_____

_____

_____

_____

_____

_____

_____

_____

_____

_____

_____

ANSWERS TO EXPLAIN, INFORM AND DESCRIBE

Question 1

Explanative texts are used to provide information that is factual, and provide details about something. An example of an explanative text includes a report explaining the importance of homework.

When you are writing to inform, you should provide the basic facts. The main difference between informing and explaining, is that explanations require more detail. A good example of an informative text is a news report, informing people of what has happened.

A descriptive text uses detailed writing to describe emotions and feelings about something or someone. An example of this could be describing a particular location or person.

Question 2

Explanation text

This is an explanation text because it is describing and explaining how something works. Texts that describe the life cycle of something are providing an account of how or why something happens in a particular way.

Question 3

This would be based on your own personal view. All you need to do for this question is to describe your perfect day.

In your writing, make sure you use detailed descriptions. You can be really creative with your response. Make sure you use strong adjectives and imagery in order to make your writing sound better.

Question 4

Explain

This extract is explaining the reasons why a person's favourite subject is P.E. It outlines several reasons as to why P.E. is their favourite, and also explains why running is their best sport.

Persuade

This extract is persuading people to choose P.E. as a subject for their GCSEs. It 'recommends' that people should invest in a good pair of trainers. It provides reasoning as to why a good pair of trainers would be beneficial.

Question 5

Informative

The text is informative as it is teaching you facts about volcanoes – it is documenting information about a particular subject. It uses technical language, facts and diagrams to inform its reader about the topic.

Question 6

Your answer should give several reasons as to why school meals should be free. Remember, explanative texts need to explain why it would be a good thing to make school dinners free for all children.

For example:

- All children will receive the same opportunities available on school premises;
- Children will receive healthy food for lunch time;
- Not all families are able to afford school dinners for their children, despite wanting them to have a hot dinner at school.
- The school will be able to promote their healthy lunch time meals, which will appeal to parents.

HOW ARE YOU GETTING ON?

THE
REVISION
SERIES

COPYEDITING
AND
PROOFREADING

COPYEDITING AND PROOFREADING

WHAT IS PROOFREADING?

By definition, proofreading is to read through a piece of written text to make sure that it is error-free.

All writers should proofread their work. This will ensure that the work is immaculate.

When proofreading, you should look out for the following:

- **Grammar;**
- **Spelling;**
- **Punctuation.**

> Allways chek four speling erors.

ERRORS:

> Allways chek four speling erors.

PROOFREAD VERSION:

> Always check for spelling errors.

A good trick when it comes to proofreading is to get someone else to read through your work. That way, you will ensure that mistakes that you haven't picked up, can be spotted by someone else.

Having a set of fresh eyes will benefit your writing.

COPYEDITING AND PROOFREADING

WHAT IS COPYEDITING?

Proofreading and copyediting are very different.

Copyediting is the process of looking over a piece of writing and making amendments to the style and language used.

<u>When editing, you should look out for the following:</u>

- Sentence structure;
- Narrative structure;
- Style of writing;
- Language used;
- Active and passive sentences;
- Consistency.

lanned for breakfast, sitting under the huge green

ich had been set up outside the café on the upper

was

ll early in the morning, the sun ^ already blazing

ze was spiced with the scent of riv life but th

rich aroma of freshly ground c

Question 1

Which of the following sentences has a mistake in its punctuation?

a) Milo was a fluffy, kitten. ☐

b) I have three brothers called Harrison, Ryan and John. ☐

c) My goldfish is yellow, pink and grey. ☐

d) My brother, Joe, is always crying. ☐

e) Although I was nervous, I did it anyway. ☐

Question 2

Which of the following sentences has a mistake in its punctuation? ☐

a) It's not a difficult task. I found it easy, fun and informative. ☐

b) "What do you want for dinner?" asked Jane. ☐

c) If it rains tomorrow I will not be happy. ☐

d) She was a tall, beautiful girl. ☐

e) My friends Ava, Sophie and Rebecca are staying the night. ☐

Question 3

Circle the correct spelling of the word in the sentences below.

a) The beautiful bride walked down the isle / aisle with her father.

b) What are you going to where / wear / were to the party tonight?

c) Simon passed / past me the plate of potatoes.

d) Their / They're / There going to be in really big trouble when they get home.

e) The dog ate two / to / too much food and now he is being sick.

Question 4

The following sentences are incorrect. Underline the word/s that is incorrect and write the correct spelling of the word/s.

a) Mia had to go and see the principle to discuss her behaviour.

_____

b) I had serial for breakfast.

_____

c) It was difficult to drive because of the missed.

_____

d) The too boys spent there day playing video games.

_____

Question 5

Below is a passage with incorrect grammar and punctuation. Read through the passage and correct the following:

- Grammar errors
- Punctuation errors
- Missing paragraphs

So far seventeen students have been placed under observation, with at least five of them at risk of temporary suspension in particular, jordans suspension was being discussed by the leadership team his bad behaviour was considered among the worst. However the greater issue at play was that none of the teachers in the science department could control the students. the head teacher has been reminded that teaching isn't purely about knowledge and the ability to put new ideas across it's equally important to be able to earn the respect of the class, and respect them in return A strong, mutual agreement between a teacher and their students is vital for success in lessons.

Mrs Brown reassured staff and parents that further training would take place to make sure teachers were able to handle the more excitable and troublesome classes Making sure that the school is a safe and efficient environment for students and teachers is still a high priority

ANSWERS TO COPYEDITING AND PROOFREADING

Question 1

A - Milo was a fluffy, kitten.

There should not be a comma in between the words 'fluffy' and 'kitten'.

Question 2

C - If it rains tomorrow I will not be happy.

For this sentence, a comma needs to be placed after the word 'tomorrow'.

Question 3

a) The beautiful bride walked down the isle / (aisle) with her father.

b) What are you going to where / (wear) / were to the party tonight?

c) Simon (passed) / past me the plate of potatoes.

d) Their / (They're) / There going to be in really big trouble when they get home.

e) The dog ate two / to / (too) much food and now he is being sick.

Question 4

a) Mia had to go and see the <u>principle</u> to discuss her behaviour.

PRINCIPAL

b) I had <u>serial</u> for breakfast.

CEREAL

c) It was difficult to drive because of the <u>missed</u>.

MIST

d) The <u>too</u> boys spent <u>there</u> day playing video games.

TWO and **THEIR**

Question 5

So far, seventeen students have been placed under observation, with at least five of them at risk of temporary suspension. In particular, Jordan's suspension was being discussed by the leadership team: his bad behaviour was considered among the worst. // However, the greater issue at play was that none of the teachers in the science department could control the students. The head teacher has been reminded that teaching isn't purely about knowledge and the ability to put new ideas across; it's equally important to be able to earn the respect of the class, and respect them in return. A strong, mutual agreement between a teacher and their students is vital for success in lessons.

Mrs Brown reassured staff and parents that further training would take place to make sure teachers were able to handle the more excitable and troublesome classes: "Making sure that the school is a safe and efficient environment for students and teachers is still a high priority."

HOW ARE YOU GETTING ON?

THE
REVISION
SERIES

STANDARD
ENGLISH

STANDARD ENGLISH

WHAT IS STANDARD ENGLISH?

Standard English refers to the English language that is widely spoken in any English-speaking country. Thus, this is deemed as the most 'normal' language used in everyday life.

This type of language is often referred to as 'the Queen's English', as it is considered the most formal way of speaking.

> "I'm gonna have a bite to eat."
>
> "I am going to have something to eat."

<u>Which of the above quotes is written in standard English?</u>

> "I'm gonna have a bite to eat."   **INFORMAL**
>
> "I am going to have something to eat."   **STANDARD ENGLISH**

- In the first quote, the use of the words 'bite' and 'gonna' suggests informal, everyday language. This is not the correct standard English.

- The second quote uses formal language and is written in its correct form. This is written in standard English.

> "What are you doing?"   **FORMAL**
>
> "Whatcha doing?"   **INFORMAL**

INFORMAL VS. FORMAL

Not only do you need to know the difference between formal and informal writing, you also need to know when to use each one.

FORMAL VS. INFORMAL

KNOWING WHEN TO USE FORMAL AND INFORMAL

In writing, you will be writing for a very specific purpose and audience. Therefore, your writing needs to be tailored to cater for the people who are going to read it.

FORMAL LANGUAGE	INFORMAL LANGUAGE
Formal language should always be used on a professional level. This type of language is great for work-related/serious speeches, news reports and emails to employers.	Informal language should be used between friends and family. This is like a 'general chat' – language you often use in everyday context. Often uses colloquialism.
Things to consider: • Keep your writing clear, and to the point. • Avoid words such as "well", "nice", "you know" etc. • Avoid friendly chat words and phrases. • Use similes and metaphors. Figurative language is great at making your writing more powerful. • Your writing needs to be clearly structured. • Avoid contracted words. • Avoid slang terminology.	This would include diary entries, emails to friends/families, informal social gatherings etc. Things to consider: • Contracted words often sound more natural. This is acceptable in informal writing. • Even with informal language, never swear! • Don't waffle on. • Informal language is often written in the way that people talk.

Question 1

For the following sentences, tick whether each sentence is written using **formal** or **informal** language.

SENTENCE	FORMAL	INFORMAL
Hi there…		
They're in real trouble		
Yours sincerely		
Dear Sir/Madam		
So, I think this should…		
It is without doubt that…		
Whatcha thinking?		
Cheers, Jamie		

Question 2

What is standard English? Give two example sentences demonstrating standard English.

_____

_____

_____

EXAMPLE 1

_____

EXAMPLE 2

_____

Question 3

Below is a draft of an email which is being sent to the head teacher. The writing used is too informal and needs to be changed. Read the email and then rewrite it using formal language.

Hi there, Mrs A,

Just thought I would drop a message to say my views on school meals. I can't afford for my son to have hot meals for lunch. But, I really want him to. Plus, all of his mates have school dinners and now he's been singled out. That's totally unfair just because I am not raking it in. So, I think we should come to some arrangement to sort this out.

Cheers,

Linda McAdam

Question 4

Which of the following (*a, b c or d*) does NOT need to be formally written?

a) An email addressed to the local council

b) A business report

c) A text message to your friend

d) A school essay

Answer [   ]

Question 5

Circle all of the words/phrases which apply to informal writing.

ENDING AN EMAIL WITH YOURS SINCERELY   **SLANG**

COLLOQUIAL LANGUAGE   **BEGINNING WITH 'DEAR'**

CONTRACTIONS   **PROFESSIONAL**   **FRIENDLY**

Question 6

Write 2 example formal sentences, 1 on how you would begin an email, and 1 how you could end the email.

EXAMPLE 1

_____

_____

EXAMPLE 2

_____

_____

ANSWERS TO STANDARD ENGLISH

Question 1

SENTENCE	FORMAL	INFORMAL
Hi there…		✓
They're in real trouble		✓
Yours sincerely	✓	
Dear Sir/Madam	✓	
So, I think this should…		✓
It is without doubt that…	✓	
Whatcha thinking?		✓
Cheers, Jamie		✓

Question 2

Standard English refers to the English language that is widely accepted in any English-speaking country. Thus, this is deemed as the most 'normal' language used in everyday life.

Please note, you could have written any two example sentences, so long as you used standard English correctly.

For example:

- She has decided to go to university.
- May I suggest a different approach?

Question 3

Your answer should be along the lines of:

Dear Mrs Anderson *(any name)*,

I am writing this email to you to express my views on school meals. I find i
difficult to afford hot school dinners for my son, and this is something I really
wish he could have.

The fact that the majority of his peers all have school dinners at lunchtime is
subjecting my son to feeling isolated. This is something I wish to amend, and
hopefully come to some arrangement with you and the school.

I know my finances are sparse, but I wish for my son to have the same
opportunities as his friends and school peers.

Thank you for taking the time to read my concerns, and I look forward to
hearing from you.

Yours sincerely,

Linda McAdam

Question 4

C - A text message to your friend

Question 5

ENDING AN EMAIL WITH YOURS SINCERELY   (SLANG)

(COLLOQUIAL LANGUAGE)   **BEGINNING WITH 'DEAR'**

(CONTRACTIONS)   **PROFESSIONAL**   (FRIENDLY)

Question 6

Example 1 – To whom it may concern / Dear Sir / Dear Madam

Example 2 – Yours sincerely, Kind regards

Your examples may be different from the above. As long as it follows the formal way of writing an email, this should be fine. Get a parent or teacher to check your examples.

HOW ARE YOU GETTING ON?

NEED A LITTLE EXTRA HELP WITH KEY STAGE 3 (KS3) ENGLISH?

How2Become have created other FANTASTIC guides to help you and your child prepare for Key Stage Three (KS3) English.

These exciting guides are filled with fun and interesting facts for your child to engage with to ensure that their revision is fun, and their learning is improved! Invest in your child's future today!

FOR MORE INFORMATION ON OUR KEY STAGE 3 (KS3) GUIDES, PLEASE CHECK OUT THE FOLLOWING:

WWW.HOW2BECOME.COM

Get Access To

FREE

Psychometric Tests

www.PsychometricTestsOnline.co.uk

Printed in Great Britain
by Amazon